VAMPIRE LESBIANS OF SODOM

and

SLEEPING BEAUTY or COMA

BY CHARLES BUSCH

D1547050

SAMUEL FRENCH, INC.

45 WEST 25TH STREET   NEW YORK 10010

7623 SUNSET BOULEVARD HOLLYWOOD 90046

LONDON   TORONTO

IMPORTANT BILLING AND CREDIT REQUIREMENTS

All producers of VAMPIRE LESBIANS OF SODOM and SLEEPING BEAUTY or COMA *must* give credit to the Author in all programs and in all instances in which the titles of the Plays appear for purposes of advertising, publicizing or otherwise exploiting the Plays and/or productions. The Author's name *must* also appear on a separate line, in which no other name appears, immediately following the title, and must appear in size of type not less than fifty percent the size of the title type.

In addition to above, the following must also appear:

"Theatre-In-Limbo, Kenneth Elliott and Gerald A. Davis presented VAMPIRE LESBIANS OF SODOM and SLEEPING BEAUTY or COMA on June 19, 1985 at the Provincetown Playhouse, New York City.

Both plays were previously presented at the Limbo Lounge in New York City in 1984."

AUTHOR'S NOTE

There are elements of fairy tales in these two one-act plays and there is a fairy tale quality to the story behind their creation. I wrote them to be performed by me and a close group of friends for one weekend in a bar called The Limbo Lounge on the lower east side of Manhattan. The performance was planned more as a party than as a professional event. The entire budget for the show was thirty six dollars. There was no stage and the lighting was composed of two sun lamps. The costumes were created from the more outlandish items in my Aunt Lillian's closet.

The act of putting on a play for the simple joy of it created a magical excitement in the room that night. We scheduled more performances and our little troupe became known as Theatre-In-Limbo. We soon developed a faithful cult audience, and it bacame clear that our "party" had commercial possibilities. We produced the show Off-Broadway. Like all good fairy tales, ours had a happy ending: a very long and prosperous run.

Along with the innocence of a fairy tale, these plays also have qualities of old fashioned burlesque sketches. They are full of opportunities for double takes, sculls, pratfalls and other comic "schtick". They should be played flamboyantly, with a sense of almost operatic intensity but more important with honesty and a sense of reality. Nothing will kill the humor of these pieces more quickly than performers who "wink at the audience" and signal that they are in on the joke.

AUTHOR'S NOTE
(continued)

In the original production, several of the female roles were played by men in drag. This is not necessary and I believe any rearrangement of gender could be successful. If men are to play some of the female roles, I think it is important that they seek out the real human qualities of these characters and not overdo their grotesqueness or bitchiness. These women are old fashioned heroines, and it's my aim that in both plays the audience should be touched by the characters renewed bond of friendship. It is that same bond of friendship that I found in Theatre-In-Limbo and which inspired this work.

PRODUCTION NOTES

Both VAMPIRE LESBIANS OF SODOM and SLEEP-ING BEAUTY or COMA were played on a bare stage. They were presented on a proscenium stage with footlights to give the feel of an old vaudeville show. I do feel that the plays could be successfully performed in a variety of stage configurations.

The backdrop for SLEEPING BEAUTY or COMA was a blow up of a page from a fashion designers' sketch pad, complete with a large swatch of fabric pinned to the drop with a giant safety pin. The sketch was of a very "mod" female fashion figure. There was also a large face of a girl with big eyes surrounded by Twiggy lashes. At key moments in the play, the eyes would close and open.

In VAMPIRE LESBIANS OF SODOM we used one back-drop that changed during each scene. In Sodom, there was a silhouette of a mountainous terrain. In Hollywood, a cut out of the Hollywood sign was placed over the mountains and in Las Vegas, a flashy sign of various gam-bling symbols covered up the Hollywood sign.

The lack of furniture and set pieces suited our shoestring budget but also allowed us to go from scene to scene with speed and fluidity.

SUGGESTED DOUBLING OF ROLES

Actor One . . . . Miss Thick, Etienne, Danny
Actor Two . . . . Enid, La Condesa
Actor Three . . . . Sebastian, King
Actor Four . . . . Fauna, Madeleine
Actor Five . . . . Ian, Oatsie
Actor Six . . . . Barry, Ali, P.J.
Actor Seven . . . . Anthea, Renee
Actor Eight . . . . Craig, Hujar, Zach

Theatre-In-Limbo, Kenneth Elliott and Gerald A. Davis presented VAMPIRE LESBIANS OF SODOM and SLEEPING BEAUTY or COMA on June 19, 1985 at the Provincetown Playhouse, New York City.

SLEEPING BEAUTY or COMA

cast

Miss Thick	Andy Halliday
Enid Wetwhistle	Meghan Robinson
Sebastian Loré	Kenneth Elliott
Fauna Alexander	Charles Busch
Ian McKenzie	Tom Aulino
Anthea Arlo	Theresa Marlowe
Barry Posner	Robert Carey
Craig Prince	Arnie Kolodner

The action takes place in and around London in the 1960's.

VAMPIRE LESBIANS OF SODOM

cast

Ali, a guard	Robert Carey
Hujar, a guard	Arnie Kolodner
A virgin sacrifice	Charles Busch
The Succubus, a monster	Meghan Robinson
King Carlisle, a silent movie idol	Kenneth Elliott
Etienne, a butler	Andy Halliday
Renee Vain, a starlet	Theresa Marlowe
La Condesa, a silent screen vamp	Meghan Robinson

VAMPIRE LESBIANS OF SODOM

cast
(continued)

Madeleiné Astarté, a stage actress . . . . . . Charles Busch
Oatsie Carewe, a gossip columnist . . . . Tom Aulino
Zack, a chorus boy . . . . Arnie Kolodner
P.J., a chorus boy . . . . Robert Carey
Danny, a chorus boy . . . . Andy Halliday
Tracy, an aspiring singer . . . . Theresa Marlowe

Synopsis of Scenes

Scene 1: Sodom, in days of old. The entrance to a forbidding cave.
Scene 2: Hollywood, 1920. La Condesa's mansion.
Scene 3: Las Vegas today. A rehearsal hall.

Scenic Design — B.T. Whitehill
Costume Design — John Glaser
Lighting Design —Vivien Leone
Prod. Stg. Mgr./Hair Des. — Elizabeth Katherine Carr
Choreography — Jeff Veazey
Directed by Kenneth Elliott

Both plays were previously presented
at the Limbo Lounge in New York City in 1984.

SLEEPING BEAUTY or COMA

SLEEPING BEAUTY or COMA

SCENE ONE

1966, London. The fashion house of Sebastian Loré (LORAY). The entire play takes place before a backdrop of a giant fashion sketch. It's a drawing of a full length fashion figure and also a close up of a girl's face with big eyes surrounded by Twiggy type lashes. MISS THICK, Sebastian's spinsterish secretary enters followed by ENID, a pretty young typist.

MISS THICK. It won't do. It simply won't do.

ENID. All the girls at the temp agency wear mini-skirts. It's the rage.

MISS THICK. Disgusting.

ENID. This is 1966, you know. It's a new age. You should get yourself a micro-mini. You've got smashing pins.

MISS THICK. If a young man ogled my loins, I'd have his eyes gouged out with a fiery poker. You've come on a very bad day. We've lost our top model and we must find a new girl by this afternoon. Mr. Loré has yet to hear the news.

ENID. Sebastian Loré. He's the top fashion designer in the world. Me lallies are turning to water.

MISS THICK. Oh pook. There's nothing to be nervous about.

(A bloodcurdling scream is heard offstage.)

Miss Thick. He's just heard about Lucinda Blake. Five, four, three, two, one, blast off!

(SEBASTIAN LORE enters. He is an older man of great stature and manic energy. He is dressed flamboyantly but in a manner redolent of a past era.)

Sebastian. How dare Lucinda Blake refuse to model my fall collection. She can't do this to me! It's a plot, I tell you. Mini-skirts, those ghastly mop headed singers, Carnaby Street. It's a plot to destroy me. Mark my words, Lucinda Blake shall regret this day.

Miss Thick. Oh Mr. Loré, not another law suit.

Sebastian. No, disembowelment. I smell a foreign presence. *(Sees ENID.)* What is this?

Miss Thick. The girl from the office temp service.

Sebastian. Cover your thighs at once, girl.

Enid. I think mini-skirts are super.

Sebastian. A woman's body must be covered from head to toe. Shackle the breasts, cinch in the waist, bind the legs. That is my fashion statement.

Enid. Aren't you going to ask my name?

Sebastian. Not likely.

Enid. Enid Wetwhistle.

Miss Thick. Miss Wetwhistle, if you would...

Enid. Enid, Miss Thick, Enid. I was named after me mum's leg waxer.

Sebastian. Such stories, your name ought to be Scheherezade. Thick, here are photos of the girls we saw last week. Perhaps one of them will do.

ENID. I don't think so. This one looks dead grotty. Grotty, grotesque. You can't have a tuned out dolly with a size ten hooter parading in such top gear rags. Ooooh, she looks like a real mixer.

SEBASTIAN. *(cooly to THICK)* The child's daft.

MISS THICK. No Mr. L., it's the new lingo, mod talk. It comes from the youth gangs, the mods and the rockers.

SEBASTIAN. My dear, do you think you could master an imitation of a deaf mute, with the emphasis on the latter?

ENID. That's very funny. Would you like me to take a letter?

SEBASTIAN. I would like you to take a personality suppressant.

MISS THICK. Mrs. Arlo should be here any minute.

SEBASTIAN. Oh yes, the very modern Anthea Arlo. She needs a gown for her anniversary. I trust that impossible sketch artist has been hard at work.

MISS THICK. Yes, Miss Alexander is indeed in the back feverishly sketching. She is quite an eccentric young lady.

SEBASTIAN. How so?

MISS THICK. Last week she told me she would like to get to know me better. She then proceeded to examine my scalp for bumps.

SEBASTIAN. Bumps?

MISS THICK. She then informed me that in a previous lifetime, I had been a cossack with a peg leg and an hyperactive penis.

SEBASTIAN. Have you seen the sketches for Mrs. Arlo?

MISS THICK. No and I don't believe they exist.

SEBASTIAN. I would like to have a word with this fanciful young lady. Bring her in.

MISS THICK. Miss Alexander, Mr. Loré would like to see you immediately. *(THICK exits.)*

ENID. I think I'm going to like working here. You're a very colorful character. I write stories in my spare time. Stories and poems.

SEBASTIAN. Do you?

ENID. Yes, perhaps someday I'll write a story about you and make a mint.

SEBASTIAN. Try it! That's all, just try it! Miss Alexander would you come in here immediately!

(FAUNA and MISS THICK enter. FAUNA is a struggling young designer dressed in an outrageous smock of her own design. She is the embodiment of the new mod look.)

SEBASTIAN. Mrs. Arlo is arriving momentarily and I understand we have no sketches to show her. Who is to blame? Surely not I. Not Miss Thick. You! You! You are to blame for this disaster and yet I suppose you want sympathy.

FAUNA. Oh yes, scads of sympathy. This has been the worst week of my entire life. *(sees ENID)* Oh my God, Clotilde!

ENID. No, I'm Enid. Enid Wetwhistle.

FAUNA. My dear, you and I were best friends a long, long time ago.

ENID. Really, when?

FAUNA. 1792. We were seamstresses in Paris during the revolution. We were involved in this royalist conspiracy and well, I hate to be the one to tell you this, we were both guillotined the same day. Hardly a groovy scene. Do you ever get neck pains?

ENID. Well, when it rains...

SEBASTIAN. I have a terrible pain in my neck.

FAUNA. Oh Mr. Loré, you and I go back even further.

SEBASTIAN. Miss Alexander, I have not time to—

FAUNA. Ancient Mesopotamia. You were my sister-in-law.

SEBASTIAN. I am flattered that you—

FAUNA. We buried you alive. You were an evil woman.

SEBASTIAN. *(exploding)* Enough! I have had enough of your addlepated lunacy. Where are those sketches?

FAUNA. *(intimidted)* Now Mr. Loré, I promise you when Mrs. Arlo arrives, you will have your sketches.

SEBASTIAN. And they better damn well be brilliant.

FAUNA. Yes sir.

(The door buzzes.)

SEBASTIAN. That must be Mrs. Arlo. Thick detain her while this nitwit gets those sketches together.

MISS THICK. Yes Mr. L. *(She exits.)*

SEBASTIAN. *(to ENID)* You, come with me. I'm about to bury you alive in a file cabinet. *(SEBASTIAN and ENID exit.)*

FAUNA. Psst!

(IAN McKENZIE pops in. IAN is a very "now" young photographer.)

IAN. Thank God, they've left. It was getting damned icy on that bloody fire escape.

FAUNA. Where are the sketches?

IAN. Here you go, luv.

FAUNA. Did you find the sketch of the dress with the popcorn balls?

IAN. It's in with the others. I hope you pull this off, luv.

FAUNA. Now all I have to do is slip my designs into the stack of Sebastian Loré sketches and pray that Anthea Arlo chooses mine.

(Offstage laughter is heard.)

IAN. I think I hear them coming. I'll get back on the fire escape.

FAUNA. I'll get the rest of the sketches.

(They exit as SEBASTIAN, MISS THICK and the glamorous ANTHEA ARLO enter. ANTHEA ARLO is a London socialite dressed in the elegantly conservative Sebastian Loré manner.)

ANTHEA. Now Sebastian darling, I don't have all day. Don't keep me in suspense, I want to see the sketches. This dress must be super spectacular. A girl celebrates her fourth second wedding anniversary only once in a lifetime.

SEBASTIAN. *(with unctuous charm)* I believe you will be quite pleased with these sketches. All arrogance aside, I am quite at the peak of my genius. Miss Thick, would you please tell Miss Alexander we're ready for the sketches. *(MISS THICK exits.)*

ANTHEA. Now you did promise me something new and extravagant. There's something vital and catching in the London air, don't you feel it?

SEBASTIAN. It's called streptococci.

(MISS THICK and FAUNA enter with the sketches.)

MISS THICK. Here they are, sir.

ANTHEA. May I? *(She takes the sketches and looks through them.)*

SEBASTIAN. The lime green crepe will look divine with the Arlo diamonds.

ANTHEA. It doesn't say anything to me. What about this one. *(She look at the next sketch.)*

SEBASTIAN. This one is quite a novelty. Notice the severity of the Bateau neck.

ANTHEA. But Sebastian, you've been showing me Bateau necks for five seasons now.

SEBASTIAN. *(haughtily)* A Bateau neckline is one of my signatures.

ANTHEA. I suppose I'm being unfair. I want you to be something you're not. My friends have been urging me to find another designer but we've had such a successful working relationship in the past.

SEBASTIAN. My dear Mrs. Arlo, do you want to go down in history as a woman of great style or do you want to be known as a flibbertygibbet who grasps onto the latest rage?

ANTHEA. I don't want to go down in history as an old fart. I'm sorry Sebastian but these will not do. Look at this gown, you've been doing variations of that same satin sheath for years. And look at...*(She flips to the next sketch and is in shock.)* Oh my...Oh my...

MISS THICK. Is something the matter?

ANTHEA. This number is spectacular. Look how short the hemline is. *(confused)* Do I dare? *(thrilled)* It's darling!

SEBASTIAN. Why, this isn't my...

ANTHEA. What's it made of?

FAUNA. Mr. Loré, that's the one you told me to in crushed velvet.

SEBASTIAN. I?

ANTHEA. I adore it. An antique fabric in a modern style. Sebastian, you are a genius. And a terribly sly fox. Oh, look at this one. A bare midriff? Where could I wear it? I'll wear it everywhere. *(Looks at another sketch.)* This is fabulous. Sebastian, what are these round balls attached to it?

FAUNA. Mr. Loré, I believe they're made of popcorn?

ANTHEA. Popcorn balls on an evening gown. I'll wear it to the opening of the Hungarian Film Festival. Sebastian, my husband will kill me but please make them all up for me. Of course, none of the the frumpy old fashioned stuff but that was meant as a joke, wasn't it?

SEBASTIAN. *(seething)* A feeble joke.

ANTHEA. I must say, a visit to your atelier is full of surprises.

SEBASTIAN. Surprises for all of us. I'll have my staff get started on all of these. Miss Thick will be calling you in two weeks for fittings.

ANTHEA. I can hardly wait. This will be so much fun. I'll leave you to your work. Sebastian, I can hardly tell you how thrilled I am for you. A whole new career shall be yours and even greater than your past.

SEBASTIAN. Miss Thick will show you out. Good day, Mrs. Arlo.

ANTHEA. Goodbye and thank you you again. *(MISS THICK and ANTHEA exit.)*

SEBASTIAN. Well, well, well, aren't we full of mischief?

FAUNA. *(frightened)* She liked the sketches.

SEBASTIAN. My new career shall be even greater than my past.

FAUNA. Does that mean you're going to let me design for your label?

SEBASTIAN. It means that I shall make those dresses for that foolish woman and then you're fired! You tried to make a fool out of me. Well, nobody makes a fool of Sebastian Loré.

FAUNA. I was just trying to get a break.

SEBASTIAN. I shall be a great help to your budding career. I shall see to it that no other fashion house will ever hire you. I suggest, my dear, you apply your ambition to another line of work.

FAUNA. *(Reaching for the sketches.)* Then I shall take my designs with me.

SEBASTIAN. Those are my designs. I believe you've forgotten the document you signed the day I took you on. All designs created under my employ are the undisputed original work of Sebastian Loré.

FAUNA. You wouldn't.

SEBASTIAN. I have. So any foolish idea of yours to contact Anthea Arlo will result in nothing more than a painful lawsuit.

FAUNA. You won't get away with this.

(IAN enters.)

IAN. Fauna, are you all right?

SEBASTIAN. And who is this young hoodlum evidentally hiding on my fire escape?

FAUNA. Ian McKenzie, my flat mate.

IAN. I overheard this entire scene and I'll make sure the papers learn how the legendary Sebastian Loré tried to destroy a young designer. You old people are all the same. You can't even see that your time is over. Fauna makes clothes that kids need to wear today, and doesn't turn them into high fashion zombies like you do.

SEBASTIAN. Miss Thick.

(MISS THICK enters.)

SEBASTIAN. Please ring the police and inform them a burglar has climbed in through our fire escape. *(THICK exits.)*

FAUNA. We're going. Come Ian. Mr. Loré, it's been perfectly enchanting working for you and I hope your fabled bateau neckline tightens and chokes you! *(FAUNA and IAN exit.)*

SEBASTIAN. Back to work. Thick, give me those composites. *(THICK enters with photos.)* We must find a new girl by this afternoon.

ENID. *(Enters with a large bolt of fabric.)* Excuse me, I found this bolt of fabric stuck away in a corner. It would make super curtains for me flat. I was wondering if you were just trashing it.

MISS THICK. *(Snatching the fabric away.)* Foolish girl, that is new fabric for the spring evening wear.

SEBASTIAN. Are you telling me that that disgusting, tawdry, loathsome fabric was ordered for my evening wear?

MISS THICK. It matches the swatches.

SEBASTIAN. No, it doesn't, you evil whore. That is not the fabric I ordered.

MISS THICK. *(Throwing it to the ground.)* I can take no more of this hysteria. I am handing in my resignation.

ENID. Oh, Miss Thick.

SEBASTIAN. You will not quit. I shall bring you to court.

MISS THICK. Bring me to court and I shall plead insanity!

SEBASTIAN. You are not mad. I am going mad! The hell with litigation, I shall murder you first!

MISS THICK. Murder away! *(SEBASTIAN chokes her.)*

ENID. Excuse me, are you trashing it then?

SEBASTIAN. Yes, yes, take the bloody lot of it! *(Calmed down, looking at photos.)* Jane Fitzhugh. Is she available for the shoot?

MISS THICK. Her libel suit against you goes to court next week.

SEBASTIAN. Gail Markham.

MISS THICK. Drying out.

(ENID drapes the fabric around herself as a way of measuring it for drapes.)

SEBASTIAN. Lisa Gardiner.

MISS THICK. Living in Pittsburgh.

SEBASTIAN. Maxine Dellafroie?

MISS THICK. Don't you remember? She's the one with the castration fantasies about you.

SEBASTIAN. No, I don't think she'll do. Tamara.

MISS THICK. Tried to poison you at last years Christmas party.

SEBASTIAN. That one has a temper. *(He notices ENID swathed in the fabric.)* Thick! Look!

MISS THICK. Where?

SEBASTIAN. There. Look what she's doing.

MISS THICK. I see nothing but an office temporary.

SEBASTIAN. She's it. She's our girl. She shall represent my fashion line around the world. Her face flashed upon a thousand magazines. Child, what was your name again?

ENID. *(in shock)* Enid Wetwhistle.

SEBASTIAN. It needs a name, a name Thick, give me a name.

MISS THICK. Let me fetch a doctor.

SEBASTIAN. She is the flower of fashion, ready to bloom. A delicate bud among thorns, waiting to be picked. A rose. A rose. That's it. From now on, my girl, you are Rose!

BLACKOUT

SCENE TWO

SEBASTIAN LORE'S fashion show. SEBASTIAN is addressing the audience.

SEBASTIAN. Ladies and gentlemen of the press, please do not stand. These past few months have been filled with fetes and festivities celebrating my twentieth anniversary as the czar of fashion. Still, I feel my greatest work is ahead of me. As I gave the women of the world a new look in 1946, today in 1966, I shall present womankind with a brand new image. And with a new image, there must be a new woman. I have found her in a young girl I call Rose. And tonight I give her to you.

(MISS THICK tiptoes out onstage, unbeknownst to SEBASTIAN. She tries to get his attention. The spotlight hits her, she freezes.)

The first number Rose will be modeling is a new adaptation of my classic satin sheath, cut on the bias, with the Loré bateau neck and a trim of gold beadwork. Note the detail of... *(SEBASTIAN turns and sees THICK and screams.)* Thick! How dare you show your face in public.

MISS THICK. Mr. L, we have a problem.

SEBASTIAN. *(whispering)* What is it? Where's Rose? *(MISS THICK whispers to him.)* What? *(She whispers again.)* I can't understand you.

MISS THICK. *(Screaming in frustration.)* She's fucking bolted!

SEBASTIAN. She's gone? *(He begins to twitch and laugh*

uncontrollably.)

MISS THICK. Mr. L, get a hold of yourself.

SEBASTIAN. Very amusing. Oh yes, this is all very amusing. A great, big joke has been played upon Sebastian Loré. *(Muttering to himself in the voice of his mother.)* Sebastian, you don't want to play with dolls. *(As himself as a child.)* Mama? Mama? *(As his cockney mother.)* I won't have you ripping apart my dresses. *(Himself as a child.)* Mama? Mama? *(as his mother)* What sort of boy is this?

MISS THICK. *(Trying to get him offstage.)* Come this way, Mr. L.

SEBASTIAN. *(in mad fury)* Get your hands off me! No one does this to Sebastian Loré. No one makes a fool of me and lives. Enid Wetwhistle, you will be sorry for this!

BLACKOUT

SCENE THREE

A wild chase ensues to the music of 1960's British rock and roll. It should have the feel of a frenetic Richard Lester film of the period. ENID runs across the stage in a plastic rain slicker. When she exits, SEBASTIAN and MISS THICK enter, one looking left, the other looking right. SEBASTIAN pantomimes for her search stage right, while he goes stage left. They exit. From stage left, three youths wearing Pierrot masks run on carrying signs saying "Down With No!" and "Now is Here!". They chant their slogans as they exit stage left. SEBASTIAN and MISS THICK enter stage left, their faces covered by open copies of the London Times. ENID enters stage right, wearing Groucho glasses with a fake nose and moustache. Not recognizing her pursuers, she taps MISS THICK on the shoulder. The two villains lower their newspapers. They too are wearing Groucho glasses. ENID makes a run for it stage right, with THICK and SEBASTIAN in hot pursuit. The youthful protesters enter stage left and cross the stage again. A strobe light begins to flicker making the stage look like a silent movie. ENID runs on from stage right followed by MISS THICK holding a butterfly net and SEBASTIAN. They circle the stage and exit right. ENID immediately enters again followed by the evil duo with this time SEBASTIAN holding the net. The protesters join them from stage right and confusion reigns. In the mayhem, ENID escapes. The protesters follow her offstage, leaving behind a foiled SEBASTIAN with only MISS THICK trapped in the butterfly net.

BLACKOUT

SCENE FOUR

FAUNA is being interviewed for a television documentary.

FAUNA. Darlings, I'm absolutely thrilled that the BBC wants to do a documentary on me but where do I start? What year? *(thoughtfully)* What century? Well, you know, I once worked for Sebastian Loré, till he fired me. Oh, those days were grim, living off tinned Ravioli, wearing my heels to flats looking for a job. Till miraculously I inherited the lease to a storefront and lo and behold, Fauna's Boutique was born. Ian was having a terrible time making a go of it as a fashion photographer. It was so unfair because his ideas were exciting and unlike anything that had been seen before.

(In a flashback, FAUNA and IAN are seen on a rainy London street. IAN is holding an umbrella.)

IAN. Oh Fauna, perhaps me Dad is right. Perhaps I'm not cut out to be a fashion photographer.

FAUNA. Darling, you're a marvelous photographer. Do't be so negative. *(Embarrassed at her bad pun.)* At least it stopped raining.

IAN. *(Putting down the umbrella.)* It's such a vicious circle. I can't get the big fashion shoots because I don't have the experience and I can't get the experience because I can't find the work.

FAUNA. If it's any comfort to you, I think you've been doing some brilliant portraiture.

IAN. I'm shooting mug shots for the penitentiary.

(ENID runs on crying, looking around furtively.)

IAN. That bird looks in trouble.

FAUNA. Ian, I know her. *(calls out)* Excuse me darling, but don't I know you from somewhere.

ENID. Oh yes. Paris, a long time ago.

FAUNA. Yes, of course, Clotilde. But I've seen you since then, haven't I?

ENID. Sebastian Loré's studio.

FAUNA. Oh yes. But where are you off to now? You look as if you were being chased by the Gestapo.

IAN. Don't be nosey, Fauna.

ENID. You're not far from the truth. After you left, Sebastian discovered me.

FAUNA. *(suspiciously)* Doing what?

ENID. No, you don't understand. He discovered me. I'm to be his top model.

IAN. You must be Rose.

FAUNA. The new mystery girl. We've read all about you in the paper. But isn't tonight your big debut?

ENID. Yes. *(She breaks down sobbing.)*

IAN. Luv, you've just got stage fright, that's all.

FAUNA. It's more than that. I can tell.

ENID. He's trying to turn me into something I'm not. He hates me, Enid Wetwhistle. It's this strange Rose character that he's obsessed with. And he wants me to live her twenty-four hours a day. I can't do it.

FAUNA. Oh, the monster.

IAN. I think I read it starts at eight. You're late already.

ENID. I can't go. Once he presents me to the press there will be no escape.

FAUNA. Don't go!

IAN. Fauna, don't get any strange ideas in your head.

FAUNA. I'm not getting them in my head. I'm feeling vibrations throughout my body. You're coming home with us. The three of us were meant to meet out here tonight. Something important and wonderful is going to happen to all of us. Where do you live?

ENID. Well, nowhere. I can't go home. He'll find me there.

FAUNA. It's too perfect. We share a flat above a Chinese restaurant. I hope you don't mind the smell of chop suey.

IAN. It's the smell of chop suey mixed with Yardley's Eau de London that's fairly nauseating.

ENID. You'd really take me in?

FAUNA. Darling, face it, you're in! *(The three turn around, their backs to the audience and are caught in a freize in silhouette.)*

BLACKOUT

SCENE FIVE

This is what is called "the happiness sequence." To the speeded up recording of Wagner's "Overture to Act III of Lohengrin", the lights come up on FAUNA skipping about joyfully holding a bouquet of flowers. IAN is holding up ENID'S legs as

they do a "wheelbarrow" walk across the stage. Blackout.
Lights come up on the trio in a pyramid formation. IAN is
stradling ENID and FAUNA'S backs. FAUNA on her
knees looks disconcerted. Blackout. Lights come up and IAN
and FAUNA are miming a tennis match with ENID the
enthusiastic fan. Blackout. Lights come up and the three are
dancing in a frenzied conga line. Blackout. The light comes
up and the three are frozen in a wacky pose. Each balanced
on one leg with their other leg extended out and arms fan-
ning out. Each one stands behind the other. They quickly lose
their balance and fall to the ground laughing at their
own foolishness.

BLACKOUT

SCENE SIX

FAUNA and IAN'S flat. FAUNA is seated on the floor painting
her nails. ENID is pacing.

ENID. Fauna, I have no direction in my life. I don't
think I even have a personality.

FAUNA. Of course you have a personality.

ENID. *(sits on the floor)* I don't know who I am. I'm a
chameleon. I take on the colors of whoever I'm with.
When I'm with you I even begin to think I'm psychic
when I'm really just your sidekick.

FAUNA. You're right. You lack direction. When I look

at you I see the number five thousand in an eastern direction.

ENID. *(blankly)* I don't know what you're talking about.

FAUNA. Now I may be off a digit but I think you should take a trip. Now it could be five thousand feet from here which I believe would land you in Trafalgar Square. But then it could be five thousand miles from here which...I wonder if there's much call for temp typists in Bora Bora.

ENID. *(Laughs and embraces FAUNA.)* Oh Fauna, I adore you. Fauna, why did you pull away?

FAUNA. Did I?

ENID. Yes, what's wrong?

FAUNA. *(extremely vulnerable)* I suddenly have this urge to kiss you. I've never felt this way about another woman.

ENID. Then kiss me. *(They tentatively move closer and gently kiss.)*

FAUNA. Oh dear, does that make me a lesbian? *(ENID holds her.)*

ENID. *(tenderly and softly)* Oh Fauna, you're not a lesbian. You're just lonely and want to be loved.

FAUNA. Yes. More than anything I want to have a baby.

ENID. Then you shall have a baby.

FAUNA. I don't know. I've had several abortions.

ENID. How many?

FAUNA. *(deadpan)* Forty-two.

ENID. Good things will happen to you. I just know it.

(IAN enters wearing his camera around his neck.)

IAN. I haven't worked in weeks. I simply must take some photos. Fauna, how about posing?

FAUNA. Darling, I'm beat.

ENID. I'll pose for you.

IAN. You would?

FAUNA. He'll want you to do nudies, he always does. It's for his art, you know.

ENID. I'll pose nude for you.

IAN. I'd never dream of asking you.

ENID. That's why I will.

FAUNA. This is my cue to pop off to Dreamland. Ta darlings. *(She exits.)*

ENID. *(calling to her)* See you in the morning. *(to IAN)* How do you want me, Ian?

IAN. Just the way you are. *(He begins clicking photos. ENID begins assuming fashion poses. IAN follows her every move.)* That's good. Great. You're a born model. Go, go, go. *(She shakes her hair seductively.)* Great! Move, move. *(She strikes more poses.)* Fabulous, move, move. *(She gets on her knees,)* Stroke yourself. *(She follows his directions.)* The hair, the face. Hand up just a bit. That's it, fabulous. *(He kisses her on the neck, then gets up.)* Come at me now. Rethink it, rethink it. *(ENID pauses for a brief moment and then removes her blouse, her back visible to the audience. She crosses her arms over her breasts.)* Fabulous. Hold it. On your back. *(She lies down, writhing on the floor.)* Keep moving. Keep working. *(IAN kneels over her body coming in closer.)* Head up towards me just a bit. *(IAN kisses her again on the neck, she caresses his thighs.)* Fabulous, more eyes, more eyes. *(IAN and ENID*

are keyed up to a pitch of excitement similar in feeling to a sex act.)
That's it! That's it! Oh my God, that's it! *(They freeze the pose
of IAN straddling her in ecstasy.)*

BLACKOUT

*(The lights come up on Fauna stage left, back in her interview with
the BBC.)*

FAUNA. That was the photo that changed out lives. Ian
sold it as a record album cover for the rock band, Dan-
delion. The record and the photo created a sensation and
sold five million copies. Everyone wanted to know who
was the mystery girl.

SCENE SEVEN

In flashback, FAUNA'S and IAN'S flat.

FAUNA. She simply has to come forth.
IAN. But what about Sebastian Loré? He must be livid
with her.
FAUNA. Soon she'll be as famous as he is. As it is, she
can't walk down the street without creating a mob scene.
She's going to need a new name. Enid Wetwhistle does
not wash with her image.
IAN. *(wearily)* How about Rose?
FAUNA. Ian, I hope you're not implying that I'm

exploiting her like that ghastly Sebastian Loré.

IAN. Don't be so sensitive.

FAUNA. Actually, Rose isn't such a bad name at that. But it's a bit too pallid, too cozy. She needs something with more bite. I've got it, Briar Rose.

FAUNA. *(at her interview)* Briar Rose became the new modeling sensation. She was signed by a top agency and soon became the highest paid international model. I was still unknown. However, when I organized my first fashion show, Rose insisted on being my runaway model. Because of her, my opening became a monster media event and my career as a designer skyrocketed. So did Ian's. His photographs of Briar Rose modeling Fauna Alexander's creation became the emblem of swinging mod London.

(FAUNA exits as ENID makes a big entrance modeling at a fashion show. She's wearing a fabulous cape which she opens and then drops to the floor. Under it, she is wearing a long tight dress. With great panache, she removes the long skirt from the dress and is now in a micro mini skirt. She picks up the long skirt, swings it over her shoulder and exits triumphantly.)

SCENE EIGHT

1969, three years later, IAN is drinking at a pub.

IAN. Who are you? Just what I thought. Another

bloody journalist. Look man, everything's been said already. The lousy scandal sheets have been full of it. Sorry mate. Sorry for jumping at you like that. I'm sure your job's none too easy. Of course, the headlines, "Wild Nights at the Top," "The True Story at Last" mean nothing. Can it be only three years since we all became rich and famous? You reporters don't know the half of it. You weren't there that night. I was. I was there and I couldn't do anything to prevent it. Anthea Arlo threw a lavish birthday party for Briar Rose at the Ad Lib Club. A night I wish I could forget.

(FLASHBACK to the party. ANTHEA enters garbed in the wildest excesses of 60's chic.)

ANTHEA. Ian, my love, don't you look smashing. I thought you'd be in Tangiers shooting the summer fashions for Vogue.

IAN. I'll let my assistants shoot Twiggy in swimsuits. A bloody bore it all is. Has Fauna arrived yet?

ANTHEA. Indeed. You can find her at the end of the bar in deep conversation with a young garment industry mogul from New York. Oh look, Julie Christie has arrived. And there's Mick and Marianne and Keith and Anita. Mick! Mick! I adored the record. Thank you! "Street Fighting Man" will be your biggest hit yet! *(to IAN)* Of course, my husband wants to melt it down for moustache wax. Bootsie's such an old fart. There's the Shrimp! I'm so pleased that Rose and Jean Shrimpton are chums and not rivals, but then that is the spirit of the times. Make love not war, n'est-ce pas? John Lennon looks quite the worse for wear. Tell me darling, do you think it's true the Beatles are splitting up?

IAN. *(Drunk and weary of ANTHEA's chatter.)* I haven't given it much thought, Anthea.

ANTHEA. I see the party began for you quite earlier.

IAN. Several days earlier in fact.

(FAUNA enters in one of her own dazzling creations accompanied by BARRY POSNER, a young New York fashion industry mogul.)

FAUNA. *(to IAN)* There you are, darling. My dear Mr. Barry Posner is dying to meet you. This young man practically runs New York's rag trade.

BARRY. Man, I really go apeshit over your work. They're not just fashion photos, but like statements about sensuality.

IAN. *(pulling her downstage right)* Fauna, I need to talk to you.

FAUNA. Can't it wait, darling?

IAN. Do you have any uppers?

FAUNA. *(annoyed)* I can't believe you are asking me this now. *(She rejoins the others.)*

BARRY. So where's the legendary Briar Rose? Isn't this her shindig?

ANTHEA. Leave it to Briar Rose to make a grand entrance at her own party.

BARRY. Fauna, honey, I am not leaving this affair without your signature. You don't know me. I'm the boy wonder of Seventh Avenue. I know from marketing. Believe me, I can do.

IAN. Believe him, he can do. Now give me some of your lovely black beauties.

FAUNA. *(to ANTHEA)* Barry wants to market a fashion line for me in the states.

IAN. You're ignoring me Fauna, I don't like it.

FAUNA. I ignore little boys when they're naughty. *(She shoots IAN a withering look.)*

ANTHEA. But your clothes are already in the finest stores in the U.S.. I've seen them.

BARRY. This is something different. These are clothes for the youth market. All synthetic and at bargain prices. And the little lady doesn't have to do bupkis. My people will design the garments. All you do is enjoy.

ANTHEA. *(looking offsage)* Oh dear, look what just walked in.

IAN. Sebastian Loré.

FAUNA. I thought you said she was dead.

IAN. That was her sister, the wicked witch of the East. She's worse than the other one was.

FAUNA. And he must be spitting bullets that his collection was such a flop.

ANTHEA. Well my dear, an entire collection of tissue paper evening gowns was bound to be a mistake.

FAUNA. He was desperately trying to be with it.

(SEBASTIAN enters in the height of outlandish mod fasion.)

SEBASTIAN. My precious darlings. Anthea, it's been ages.

ANTHEA. Good evening Sebastian. I do hope you've come here in the spirit of friendship.

SEBASTIAN. Friendship of the purest nature. My dearest darling Fauna. *(Kisses her.)* Now Mr. McKenzie, you may kiss me. Don't be afraid. Think of me as you would a kindly old Aunt. *(They kiss.)*

FAUNA. Sebastian, this is Barry Posner. Sebastian Loré.

BARRY. Are you in the industry?

SEBASTIAN. *(laughs)* On the fringe, dear boy. But where is our lovely Rose, our Briar Rose?

ANTHEA. I wonder what could be keeping her.

(BRIAR ROSE (ENID) enters in the wildest outfit and coiffure of all.)

SEBASTIAN. Ah, the goddess emerges.

ANTHEA. Happy birthday darling.

ENID. Thank you so much for throwing this party.

FAUNA. Darling. You look lovely. *(They kiss.)*

IAN. Hello, luv.

SEBASTIAN. Remember me?

ENID. *(startled)* Mr. Loré...

SEBASTIAN. Don't say a word. All of our problems are in the past. I come only to celebrate you.

ENID. You don't despise me for walking out on you?

SEBASTIAN. How can I despise someone for grabbing a better opportunity. I would have done the same thing meself at a younger age. As a matter of fact, I'd like to make a toast to the modern Aphrodite—

ANTHEA. *(With wild enthusiasm, sees someone out front.)* Could it be? It couldn't. It is! It's Garbo!

EVERYONE. Garbo!

(FAUNA, IAN, SEBASTIAN and BARRY join ANTHEA to gaze upon Garbo. ENID looks at her from stage left. Unseen by all, MISS THICK, SEBASTIAN'S secretary, tiptoes out carrying a black box marked LSD. Without ENID noticing, MISS THICK pours some of the LSD into the drink in ENID's outstretched hand and scurries off.)

ANTHEA. *(Seeing it's not Garbo.)* Well, it looked like her. *(The group moans in disappointment.)*

SEBASTIAN. As I was saying. A toast to the incomparable Briar Rose.

EVERYONE. Cheers! *(They all drink.)*

FAUNA. *(to ENID)* Darling, I heard all about the Schlesinger film. You're really switched on.

BARRY. Excuse me for interrupting but I'm not giving up. Fauna, name your price and then hows about dancing with me.

FAUNA. Name my price? That's more like it, boy wonder. Let's dance. *(They do a strenuous dance number and everyone joins in. At the end of the number, ENID begins to feel the effect of the LSD and screams.)*

ENID. *(stares at FAUNA)* Fauna, your face is turning into the most peculiar pattern of paisley.

FAUNA. The lighting is rather grim but...

ENID. What's wrong with your nose? It keeps growing longer. Get it away from me before you sneeze.

ANTHEA. Is this a new lingo?

IAN. Luv, are you all right?

ENID. I don't know. I feel like I'm on a rollercoaster

that's flying off the track. Coo, Mick Jagger's lips are getting so huge. I bet I could bounce off them like a trampoline.

SEBASTIAN. I think the dear girl's drunk too much.

IAN. It's not alcohol. She's tripping on LSD!

SEBASTIAN. Perhaps we should get her home.

ENID. *(to SEBASTIAN)* It's the wicked witch! Get her away from me! She turns young girls into department store manniquins. Get her away from me!

SEBASTIAN. She's quite fanciful, isn't she? Come, dear.

ENID. No, I'm not going with you! I know what you want. I won't do it! I won't let you drain my life away! Get away! Get away from me! *(She sinks to the floor.)*

FAUNA. *(frantic)* Oh my God, she's unconscious.

IAN. I've never seen this happen before.

FAUNA. *(holding ENID)* Quick, someone call a doctor. Anthea, hurry! *(ANTHEA screams in panic.)*

BLACKOUT

IAN. *(back at the pub)* She never woke up. The doctors said it was a strange mixture of LSD that induced the coma. In effect, Fauna and I slipped into the coma with her that night. I haven't shot another photograph. Fauna sold everything and went into seclusion. Dammit, don't you realize the sixties are over!

(The giant eyes of the fashion drawing on the backdrop close.)

BLACKOUT

SCENE NINE

The present. CRAIG PRINCE, a handsome young nutritionist is being interviewed by a health magazine.

CRAIG. What's the name of your magazine? "Natural High?" Of course, I'm sorry. This book tour has been amazing. A different city every day, radio shows, newspaper interviews. I'm not complaining. Only two years ago people thought I was a nut harping on these wierd theories about vitamins and nutrition. I guess 1986 is my year. Basically I'm blown away that there's been so much media attention to my book "Eating Right is the Best Revenge." I know what you want me to talk about so I'll get that over with first. I'll just start at the beginning again. I came to London in June 1984. A good friend of mine, Clive, was ill and I went to visit him at a small sanitarium. It was a creepy place. It looked like an old castle, probably was one at one time. Well, I have one lousy sense of direction and I must have turned the wrong corner and I found myself in a completely different wing. Very still and very empty. I looked around for a nurse or anyone to help me find my way out. At the end of the corridor was an open door and a strange figure in black. I assumed it was a nun.

(FLASHBACK. FAUNA garbed in a black cape and hat with a veil brings on the comatose ENID in a wheelchair.)

CRAIG. Excuse me.

FAUNA. *(taken by surprise)* Who are you?

CRAIG. I'm sorry, I thought you were someone else.

FAUNA. How did you get in here?

CRAIG. I'm lost. This place is like a maze.

FAUNA. Please go.

CRAIG. Who is she? She's so beautiful.

FAUNA. Enid Wetwhistle.

CRAIG. I've seen that face before. What happened to her?

FAUNA. A bad acid trip. She's been in a coma for fifteen years.

CRAIG. I'm a nutritionist. I can tell many things about a person merely be pressing certain vitamins in their hands. I can instantly tell what elements their system is lacking. *(CRAIG takes vitamins out of his pocket and presses them in ENID'S hand.)* She could use some super B's. As well as a good dose of D and E. Lecithin would help and Lysine and some pure bioflavonoids. You'll probably think I'm a nutcase but I've been experimenting with Llama enzymes and that might just do it for her. Let me work on this. *(FAUNA exits.)*

(In the present.) Well, I did. I worked hard. I was obsessed by that silent face. I returned the following week and when the doctors and nurses weren't looking I injected her with a megadose of fifty-eight different vitamin and mineral combinations, as well as some high density Llama enzymes.

(In the past.) Oh Sleeping Beauty, will nothing disturb your eternal slumber? *(He injects her and kisses her. She awakes. The eyes on the backdrop open as well.)*

ENID. Where are the Beatles? I heard all four of them were coming to the party.

CRAIG. That party's over. A new one's about to begin.

ENID. Who are you?

CRAIG. Craig Prince. What's your name?

ENID. Briar Rose...No, Enid Wetwhistle...No, Briar Rose. Briar Rose and Enid Wetwhistle. I suppose they're one and the ᵢme. How very strange and sort of wonderful. I think I d like to stretch my legs. I must say, I've certainly had a good night's sleep. *(She exits.)*

CRAIG. *(In the present.)* With Briar Rose restored to life, I then brought back to life her two friends, Ian McKenzie and Fauna Alexander, two leading figures of the swinging sixties. I converted them all to my philosophy of nutrition and enzyme action and now they're all on tour with me plugging my book and video tapes.

(IAN enters dressed in the height of new wave fashion.)

IAN. Yup, we're all on the comeback trail. Craig made me realize that my drug and drinking habits were largely due to a severe case of hypoglycemia. For the first time in years, I can really see clearly. I've just shot the entire December issue of Vogue and I'm about to start directing a big budget music video starring non other than Briar Rose and costumed by Fauna Alexander.

(FAUNA enters dressed in the epitome of outrageous contemporary chic.)

FAUNA. Ian is right. We owe so much to Craig and his

Llamas with their miracle enzymes. For the first time I'm not ashamed to admit that for many years, I was suffering from Anorexia Bulemia. Craig has cured me of that terrifying disease. I'm also developing a new perfume with a Llama base as well as opening four "Fauna's Boutiques" in New York, Los Angeles, Tokyo and Palm Springs. We've regained the spirit of youth.

(ENID enters. She too is costumed in the high fashion style of today.)

ENID. And then of course, I's still be fast asleep if it wasn't for Craig. He's bringing me to Ho-Ho-Kus, New Jersey next week to meet his mum.
CRAIG. Shall we tell them the happy news?
ENID. Craig and I are going to be married.
FAUNA. I also have some important news. I'm going to have a baby.
IAN. And I'm the lucky dad.
ENID. My dear friends, I'm so happy for you.
FAUNA. And I'm so happy for you.
IAN. I'm happy too.
CRAIG. So am I. I guess we have it all.

(SEBASTIAN and MISS THICK enter in dirty rags.)

SEBASTIAN. You may wonder what became of Sebastian Loré and Miss Thick. We punished ourselves with our own guilt. And so we emigrated to Guatemala where we pick papayas to feed the poor. Only last week, I unearthed a tattered copy of People Magazine and there I read that Rose and Craig and Fauna and Ian were all living quite happily ever after.

(The two romantic couples are holding hands. IAN turns to look at CRAIG and they wink. They go back to their gals and kiss. The lights blackout. The lights flash on again rather like a photographers flashbulb catching the couples in amused surprise.)

BLACKOUT

VAMPIRE LESBIANS
OF SODOM

VAMPIRE LESBIANS OF SODOM

PROLOGUE

Sodom in days of old. Two GUARDS are standing sentry before the entrance to a forbidding cave.

ALI. Who goes there?

HUJAR. You needn't fear Ali. No one ventures near this spot save for madmen and fools.

ALI. Including you and me.

HUJAR. Yes, but we are clever fools. For our deed today, we shall receive a kingly sum.

ALI. If we live to spend it.

HUJAR. The creature we guard desires nothing of the likes of you. The Succubus thrives upon the blood of young virgins.

ALI. A rare delicacy, eh?

HUJAR. You must be new to these parts. Where do your people hail from?

ALI. I hail from Ishbar, in Asia Minor. You know, the fertile crescent.

HUJAR. So what brings you to Sodom?

ALI. Don't scoff, but I've come to seek my fortune.

HUJAR. Then my friend, you've made a wise move. This city has everything. It never sleeps. Have you been to the bars?

ALI. No, I'm living out in Gommorah.

HUJAR. Gommorah?

ALI. Hujar, I don't want to offend you but I'm really not into bars. I'm looking for a relationship.

HUJAR. Then my man, you shouldn't have moved to the twin cities.

(A cock crows.)

HUJAR. The cock has crowed. It's time to begin. The Succubus demands its breakfast.

ALI. Have you ever seen the Succubus?

HUJAR. No one has, except for the virgin sacrifice and obviously, they never live to tell. We had best begin. The sleeping potion will wear off, the virgin will awake and we'll have a lot of explaining to do. You wait here. I'll bring her in.

(He exits. HUJAR returns carrying in his arms the beautiful young virgin.)

HUJAR. Quite a beauty, isn't she? A pity she is to be sacrificed.

ALI. Hujar, she stirs.

HUJAR. That cannot be. The potion should last an hour more. Damn the Gods, let's get out of here. *(The GIRL begins to wake in his arms.)*

GIRL. No, Papa, I don't want to play. Please, don't make me. *(She awakes.)* Where am I? Who are you? Please sir, release me. *(He puts her on her feet. The virgin is indeed beautiful but there is something about her costume and demeanor that suggests a stripper performing a burlesque sketch about vestal virgins. It could be the G-string and spike heels.)*

HUJAR. We are soldiers under the command of the Governor.

GIRL. My mind is such a jumble. I had such a strange dream. I dreamt there was a lottery to choose a sacrificial victim for the dreaded Succubus and I dreamed that I chose the black stone of death. You know, they say our dreams can be interpreted. They can tell us many things about ourselves. I wonder what this dream means.

HUJAR. That was no dream, that was the truth. You are the virgin sacrifice.

GIRL. *(Thinks they're joking.)* You couldn't be...but surely you...no, I...I couldn't...It's imposs...*(She realizes it's true and screams. HUJAR grabs her around the neck.)*

HUJAR. Another peep out of you and we'll rip your tongue out.

ALI. Hujar, be kind to the girl. These are her last moments on earth.

HUJAR. And they shall be ours if her screams bring forth the Succubus. *(ALI breaks HUJAR'S arm away.)*

GIRL. Please sir, I beg of you. If there is any shred of pity or tenderness in your heart. Please, do not deliver me to the Succubus.

HUJAR. We only follow our orders.

GIRL. *(to ALI)* You, you have the eyes of a poet. Surely you cannot see it just to send me to this most horrible of deaths.

ALI. I wish there was something I could do.

HUJAR. Soldier, control yourself. You are acting weak and womanish.

GIRL. If having a kind heart is womanish, be proud of

your womanhood. I implore you, sir, save me. My father has money. Aid my escape and all of his gold shall be yours.

HUJAR. Child, you have been forsaken. Your father has publicly announced his pride in your selection as food for the Goddess.

GIRL. I refuse to believe this.

ALI. It's true. We have his sworn testimonial of acceptance.

GIRL. Then it is true. I am truly alone. A mere child of fourteen. Friendless, parentless, damned to this most vile fate. Tell me, my good executioners, how much time do I have?

HUJAR. But a few minutes more.

GIRL. Then permit me a moment whilst I bid farwell to my girlhood. *(In a reverie.)* Goodbye youth. Adieu bubbling brook of joy, rosy hope of budding romance. I bid farewell to the frothy games of catching a whip o'whill and skipping to it's tune, lightening bugs parading their brilliance before the first evening stars. I wave goodbye to the beardless boys who breathlessly snatched a forbidden kiss and the silly girls who giggled at my follies. Goodbye dear friends. Farewell round orb.

ALI. Is there nothing I can do to ease your pain?

GIRL. Yes, there is something you could do. Break my hymen. Rape me and I'll no longer be a virgin fit for sacrifice.

ALI. But, I.... *(The GIRL rips off ALI'S loincloth and chases him around screaming "Break my hymen, break my hymen!" HUJAR pushes her to the ground.)*

HUJAR. The child is mad. Away! *(The two soldiers exit.)*

GIRL. I beseech thee Isis, provide me with the courage to face my destruction.

(The SUCCUBUS enters in the form of a beautiful and very hardboiled dame. She is by turns very grand and also a bit cheap but most importantly, she has a very big chip on her shoulder.)

GIRL. Run! Save yourself! The creature is about to emerge.

SUCCUBUS. *(irritated)* Hey, hey, hey! Where are you going?

GIRL. Woman, have you lost your senses?

SUCCUBUS. Not that I'm aware of.

GIRL. Who are you?

SUCCUBUS. Give a guess.

GIRL. An actress?

SUCCUBUS. Guess again.

GIRL. Are you a courtesan?

SUCCUBUS. I am the Succubus that you've heard tell about.

GIRL. How can pure evil be embodied by such beauty?

SUCCUBUS. How much easier to lure you into my arms. Come, child.

GIRL. Vile thing, what right have you to demand my death?

SUCCUBUS. *(angrily)* Do I not also have the right to life? As you need food and water so I need the pure unsullied blood of virgins.

GIRL. What proof have you of my maidenhead? What if I told you I was the village slut, a repository for every man's seed in Sodom?

SUCCUBUS. I'd say you were a big fat liar. Now you tax my patience, child. Come.

GIRL. I'm afraid to die.

SUCCUBUS. *(with great self pity)* That's nothing to be afraid of. Think how much crueler my fate, never to die, condemned to immortality. The perennial witness to the eternal passing parade. My cave is quite the lonely one.

GIRL. Forgive me if I don't weep.

SUCCUBUS. A spitfire, eh. But why should you pity me? I suppose you look at me now and imagine I'm quite a glamorous, flamboyant creature. In your ignorance, you fancy my life to be one of extravagance and magic. How wrong you are. Yes, I have my slaves that do my bidding but they are semi-human primitive creatures and far from scintillating dinner companions. True, my cave is overflowing with sparkling jewels, but where the fuck can I wear them? My life stinks. The only enjoyment I get is a vestal virgin now and then. But time goes on and I survive and how? How you may wonder do I face the prospect of a millenium of time on my hands? What keeps me going is a sense of humor. I look for small inconsequential things that will provide me with amusement and so far, in that department, my fair young lady, you're not racking up any gutbusters.

GIRL. You play at human feeling, but you possess as much humanity as the dragons at sea.

SUCCUBUS. Child, I must say I am impressed by your fortitude. If you were a fellow Succubus, I might even be afraid of you. But you are not. You will look into my eyes and all thought of defiance shall vanish. Look into my eyes. Look into my eyes. Look into my eyes! *(The GIRL is hypnotized by the SUCCUBUS.)* You will come to me now. *(very imperiously and most unseductively)* Seek out my warmth. Suckle at my breast.

GIRL. *(Crosses to the SUCCUBUS.)* Yes, yes, protect me, dear mother. *(The SUCCUBUS lunges toward the GIRL and drinks her blood ravenously.)*

BLACKOUT

SCENE TWO

Hollywood, 1920. The drawing room of LA CONDESA'S spectacular mansion high in the Hollywood hills. KING CARLISLE, a handsome, young matinee idol is pacing back and forth. ETIENNE, LA CONDESA'S extremely nervous butler enters.

ETIENNE. Young man, you will have to leave at once. Madame La Condesa is incommunicado.

KING. You have kept me waiting for over an hour. I demand to see La Condesa. Why won't she see me?

ETIENNE. Madame is ruled by her caprices.

KING. This is intolerable. Sir, don't you know who I am?

ETIENNE. Are you here to fix the victrola?

KING. I take it you never go to the movies.

ETIENNE. I only see Madame's films.

KING. I am King Carlisle, the newest and biggest male star in silent pictures. She can't treat me this way.

ETIENNE. My good man, only yesterday Madame received Winston Churchill, Monsieur Diaghilev and the King of Spain. King Carlisle? Small potatoes.

KING. Well, Monsieur Le Butler, I consider your mistress even smaller potatoes. Furthermore, I am not impressed by her phoney title, Madame La Condesa Scrofula de Hoya, indeed. Surely she knows that the studio has brought the great stage actress, Madeleine Astarté out to Hollywood and is grooming her as Magda's rival.

ETIENNE. Magda Legerdemain is a great artist with the divine spark, Madeleine Astarté: pure hambone.

KING. You must help me. I have nothing against your mistress. I merely wish to save my fiancée Renee from her clutches. Renee is an innocent. She is new to Hollywood. She doesn't recognize corruption when she sees it. I must save her from La Condesa.

ETIENNE. What have you to fear?

KING. There are so many rumors surrounding Magda Legerdemain. Rumors that she's not only a vamp but...a vampire.

ETIENNE. Excuse me, I must go. It's time to run Madame's leopards in Griffith Park. *(He tries to leave. KING stops him.)*

KING. You're hiding something from me.

ETIENNE. *(screams)* Don't touch me! I will tell you this. You have entered a mad household. This isn't hair on my head, these are nerve endings.

KING. Then why do you work here?

ETIENNE. Who else but Madame would employ me? You don't recognize me, do you?

KING. No, who are you?

ETIENNE. Suffering has changed my face as completely as a surgeon's scalpel. I will tell you this, Baby Kelly Ambrose lives!

KING. Surely you're not Baby Kelly Ambrose, the hatchet wielding vaudeville child star.

ETIENNE. *(Breaks into a timestep and swings an imaginary hatchet.)* I did them all in after a milk fund benefit in Kokomo. I dismembered all six of them and scattered their body parts along the entire Keith-Orpheum circuit. Only one person would aid my escape from the lunatic asylum and that was La Condesa and for her sake, I would gladly strike again.

KING. Oh dear, I must remove Renee from this bedlam.

(RENEE VAIN runs on and speaks to ETIENNE. RENEE is a lovely ingenue in the Mary Pickford mode but with the toughness of a Ma Barker.)

RENEE. Etienne, La Condesa would like...*(sees KING)* King, what on earth are you doing here?

KING. My dearest darling, I'm here to talk some sense into you.

RENEE. Please, go away. You don't understand.

KING. I understand all too well.

RENEE. *(with mad vitality)* No, you don't. You want me to lead a quiet, dreary life as your wife. Well, that's not why I came to Hollywood. I want to live! I want to drive my roadster faster than anyone else on the road. I want to stay up all night, drinking whiskey and dancing on table tops. *(laughs with wild abandon)* I'm young, let me be reckless!

KING. My darling, I fear for you.

RENEE. Etienne, could you leave us alone for a moment?

ETIENNE. If you think that's wise. (He exits.)

RENEE. *(as tough as nails)* King, you nincompoop, you're going to spoil everything. This dame's my entree to the big wigs in this burgh. She knows everyone. We had breakfast with Wallace Reid, lunch with Alma Rubens, tea with Clare Kimball Young and dinner with Rod La Rocque. This place is a social gold mine and I'm reaping in the nuggets. I got me three screen tests lined up for next week.

KING. But I know people. I could help you.

RENEE. *(distainfully)* Oh, a lot of help you are. You got me tossed off the DeMille picture. You didn't think I knew that, did you?

KING. The role was cheap and degrading.

RENEE. Let me be cheap and degraded, I'm an actress! I've had enough of you butting into my career, you great big buddinsky! *(He reaches for her.)* Don't touch me. You repulse me. When I think of your feeble attempts to make love to me, I laugh. Do you hear me, I laugh. *(Explodes in hysterical laughter.)*

KING. *(Shakes her violently.)* Stop it! Stop it! This isn't you, this isn't my Renee.

RENEE. *(suddenly lovely and vulnerable)* King, I don't know what came over me. That was a different girl speaking. Some strange power overtook me and made me say those cruel words. Can you forgive me?

KING. Of course darling. I must get you out of this mansion. Can't you smell the presence of evil?

(La CONDESA [la CONDAYSA] enters garbed in the barbaric excesses of silent screen vamps. She is of course the SUCCUBUS from Sodom looking not a day older.)

LA CONDESA. Mr. Carlisle, you smell the presence of evil? Perhaps you are mistaking it for my perfume. If you are, it's expensive evil, fifty dollars an ounce. Now state your business.

KING. I demand that you give up Renee.

LA CONDESA. *(with flamboyant levity)* Give her up? I see no handcuffs, I see no chains.

KING. I believe she is under your spell. I've heard tales of the stream of young girls who pass through these portals. Young starlets who are never heard of again. Where are those starlets?

LA CONDESA. *(very grandly)* If you must know, I give them private coaching. I audition them and I give them an honest appraisal of their talent. Can I help it if they all go back to Wichita?

RENEE. Tonight she's going to teach me how to play a passionate love scene.

KING. I can't bear this torment. Don't you know what she is?

RENEE. A very nice lady.

KING. *(with self righteous fury)* This very nice lady drinks the blood of young virgins. Yes, I know the truth about you, Madame La Condesa. I know you had to flee Europe because of the rumors of your evil ways. And here you are corrupting every virgin in Hollywood.

LA CONDESA. Slim pickings I must say. If I were interested in virgins, why the hell would I come to Hollywood? My friend, you've seen too many motion pictures.

KING. I am not your friend. I spit on your friendship! *(He spits on the floor.)*

LA CONDESA. *(mad as a hornet)* Spit on my friendship but not on my rug!

KING. I will, I will if that will save my Renee. *(spits several times)*

LA CONDESA. *(with great vulgarity)* You clam up one more time and there's gonna be hell to pay. Etienne! Clean up this mess. *(ETIENNE runs in.)* Now look here you...

ETIENNE. Madame, Miss Carewe from the Hearst newspapers will be here momentarily. Don't you think you should be composing yourself?

LA CONDESA. Yes, I must compose myself before that nosy bitch arrives. Mr. Carlisle, the door is that way.

KING. I am not leaving. I shall be here when Oatsie Carewe arrives and I shall provide her with some juicy gossip for her column.

RENEE. *(angrily)* You wouldn't!

ETIENNE. Madame, shall I call the police?

LA CONDESA. No, let him stay. And let him repeat this slander. It shall only add fuel to my legend.

(Doorbell rings.)

LA CONDESA. That must be Miss Carewe. Show her in, Etienne. *(ETIENNE exits.)*

RENEE. King, I wish you would get the point that you're not wanted here. *(ETIENNE enters.)*

ETIENNE. Madame Madeleine Astarté.

LA CONDESA. *(aghast)* Astarté!

RENEE. What's she doing here?

LA CONDESA. Tell her to go away. Tell her I'm not receiving.

(MADELEINE ASTARTE [ASTARTAY] enters in the grand manner. She is none other than the virgin from Sodom, now the dazzling grande dame of the New York stage.)

MADELEINE. Balderdash, La Condesa. I've traveled all the way from New York just to see you.

LA CONDESA. You must not flatter me. All Hollywood knows of your million dollar contract.

MADELEINE. *(with gaity)* Million point five. The point five darlings is to keep me in mascara. *(Laughs and looks at ETIENNE next to her. She does a big burlesque double take at his deadpan expression.)*

LA CONDESA. Madame Astarté, I would love to offer you tea but unfortunately I'm expecting Oatsie Carewe any minute for an in depth profile.

MADELEINE. Oh, I must stay for that. I do so want to get to know you better. Besides this will dispell all those awful rumors that we're rivals. How absurd, you and I rivals. We couldn't possibly play the same roles. Perhaps mother and daughter.

LA CONDESA. *(lightly bitchy)* Dear, you look entirely too young to play my mother.

MADELEINE. Aren't you kind, Contessa.

LA CONDESA. *(Cordially correcting her.)* Condesa *(CON-DAYSA)* Madeleine, if I may be so familiar, have they chosen your first vehicle?

MADELEINE. Yes, I'm to do the life of Madame DuBarry.

LA CONDESA. This is an outrage! I am to play DuBarry. My costumes are all made.

MADELEINE. We had to take in the waist a little. Lay off the paté, Cunt-tessa.

LA CONDESA. *(angrily)* Condesa! *(CONDAYSA)*

MADELEINE. After the DuBarry picture I shall do the life of Mary Magdalene.

LA CONDESA. You little bitch, that was supposed to be my follow-up picture.

MADELEINE. Dear heart, I do hope you won't mind but the studio felt they needed a real actress for the role.

LA CONDESA. This is shear treachery and you won't get away with this! *(turns to leave)*

KING. Madame Astarté, she has the devil on her side.

LA CONDESA. I'll fix you, I'll fix you by all the powers that be!

RENEE. What will you do?

LA CONDESA. *(with intense frustration)* I'm calling my agent! *(She exits.)*

ETIENNE. Oh dear! *(follows her out)*

KING. Madeleine, I fear for your life. You may think me mad but I have reason to believe LaCondesa is one of the undead.

MADELEINE. No darling, she just looks like death. *(to RENEE)* But you, my dear, you look much livelier. I don't believe we've met.

RENEE. My name is Renee Vain. I'm a new contract player at the studio.

MADELEINE. How perfectly devine. You have such a lovely face. Profile. Ah, yes.

KING. We're engaged to be married.

MADELEINE. Pish posh. An actress must be married to her art. Men, ugh. *(shudders)* Thespis shall be your lover.

RENEE. That's what La Condesa says.

MADELEINE. Does she? I suppose you and LaCondesa are quite intimate.

RENEE. I love her so much.

MADELEINE. Yes, an older woman can be such a comfort to a young girl. I can tell you are a superb actress and we must play together. I know the perfect vehicle. I've just optioned a new book on an old subject. The story of Sapho. I play Sapho, a noble Greek woman, passionate, vibrant, a sexual revolutionary and you, my fair one, you shall play her lesbian lover...*(searches for a name)* Rusty.

RENEE. Rusty?

MADELEINE. I can see the scene. The cameraman lining up the shot. The director calls "Action", the off screen violinist commences to play. Sapho see Rusty coming out of the Parthenon, the wind tossing her hair away from her face. Sapho slips her arm around Rusty's waist and silently they...

RENEE. But I don't...

MADELEINE. I said silently, they walk down a dark winding street. It's the street where Sapho lives with her grandmother, Ruchel. The street is empty. Everyone being at the Olympic games. They look into each other's eyes. Rusty finds herself yielding to the older woman's incandescent beauty. Cameras pan in for a tight shot. They kiss. *(They kiss and then ASTARTE bites RENEE'S neck until the girl faints.)* Kill the lights, call it a wrap.

KING. *(in shock)* You...you...you're a vampire!

MADELEINE. I don't suppose you have a handkerchief.

KING. She devil! Fiend! You've killed my Renee.

MADELEINE. Nah, she'll come to, but lets say I've taken the bloom off the peach.

KING. I'll expose you, I'll expose you as the monster you are.

MADELEINE. *(cooly)* I wouldn't talk about exposing anyone if I were you.

KING. What do you mean?

MADELEINE. I happen to know King Carlisle's not your real name.

KING. So, many stars change their names.

MADELEINE. I happen to know your real name is Trixie Monahan and before you came to Hollywood, you worked as what is politely called a model/escort with a strictly male clientele. Trixie Monahan, I'll expose you as a homosexual.

KING. *(dissolving into tears)* Yes, it's true, it's true. I am, I am.

MADELEINE. You may one day marry and even have children but you will always be a homosexual, *(with mon-*

strous ferocity) ALWAYS!

KING. Then there's nothing left for me to do but kill myself.

MADELEINE. There are other alternatives.

KING. Such as?

MADELEINE. You can be my personal slave.

KING. What would you expect of me?

MADELEINE. Lots of things. Escort me to premieres, wash my car, rinse out my dirty panties, but don't you dare let me catch you wearing them. I get plenty mad.

(He collapses into depair. LA CONDESA enters.)

LA CONDESA. What is this? What have you done to her? Now you've really gone too far. You imagine yourself quite the cunning vixen. You have delusions that you can conquer me. Though I have always found you vulgar, I have never taken you for a fool, until now. Hollywood is my town. For centuries, you have been an albotross around my neck. First in Rome, I claimed as my bride, the most beautiful of Caligula's courtesans. She was mine until you stole her away to China. Then there was the nun in the dark ages who became my personal slave, stolen once again. We all know what treachery you conspired against me during the Spanish Inquisition but I triumphed. And did I plot revenge? No. Then in the sixteenth century, I had as my mistress, the most desired of Queen Elizabeth's ladies in waiting. You, the ever present vulture snatched her off to the colonies. Even then, did I choose revenge? No. And why? Because I am a great lady. I conduct myself with dignity and grandeur whilst you roll in the gutter, parading your twat onstage and calling it acting. You've got as much glamour as a common street whore and now madame, you have gone too far. I am the queen of vampires and I shall never, never relinquish my hold on Hollywood!

MADELEINE. Are you through? As you desire to relive the past, shall we travel even further back in time. Many centuries ago, back in the days of the Bible, there was a young girl, a mere child of fourteen, a lovely girl, full of high spirits. A lottery was held to choose a sacrificial victim for the dreaded Succubus. As fate would have it, she chose the black stone of death. She was dragged by soldiers to the cave of the creature and there left to her desecration. The monster emerged and there under a Godless sky, the creature dug her teeth into the girl's fair flesh. Having gorged itself, the monster retired to its cave, leaving the girl's body to be pecked and devoured as carrion. But the girl did not die. The monster in its fury did not even notice that all the while it was sucking the girl's blood, the child herself had lodged her teeth into a vein of the monster. In her terror she drank. More and more she filled herself with the creature's fluid. And there on that bleached rocky point, left to rot like a piece of old meat, the girl did not die but was transformed, transformed into one of the undead, never to find eternal rest but to stalk the earth forever in search of a victim, forever alone, forever damned. Look at me, I am that girl! And I demand the death of the Succubus!

(ETIENNE enters.)

ETIENNE. Miss Oatsie Carewe of the Hearst Newspapers.

(OATSIE CAREWE enters.)

OATSIE. Darling! And Madeleine Astarté too. What a marvelous surprise. Who'd have thought you two gals would be chums. And they say Hollywood is a heartless town. Magda, I adore the dress. It does wonders for your figure, so concealing. And Madeleine, I just know that must be a Paris creation. I must have a description of it for my column.

LA CONDESA. Oatsie darling, may I get you some tea?

OATSIE. No, no, never touch the stuff. Okay girls, straight from the hip, how did this feud rumor begin?

LA CONDESA. What feud? I adore Madeleine. I've adored her for what seems like centuries.

OATSIE. *(sees KING and RENEE)* What's this? King Carlisle, Renee Vain, two stars of tomorrow.

MADELEINE. Do you know this wonderful lady spends her free time coaching young actors. They were just performing a scene for us and are totally exhausted. Such is the dramatic art.

LA CONDESA. Oh yes, she knows. It's not all glamour.

MADELEINE. So true, so true. Particularly when you act, Magda. Such shattering realism. Why you're more than realistic, you're nearly grotesque.

LA CONDESA. Thank you, dear.

OATSIE. Madeleine, I want to give you a real Hollywood welcome. I just insist you come to my house for dinner. I'm a demon in the kitchen and you come too, Magda, I insist. What shall I make? A goulash. Yes, a nice thick goulash, a native dish of Transylvania. Have you ever been there, Magda?

LA CONDESA. No, I don't believe I've ever been to Transylvania. No doubt Madeline has been there on one of her theatrical tours.

MADELEINE. No, I've never played Transylvania. Altonna, yes, Transylvania, no.

OATSIE. I adore a good goulash, spiced with plenty of garlic. I hope you don't have an aversion to garlic.

LA CONDESA. No, no, the hotter the better. Remember, I was once married to a Spanish nobleman, the Count Scrofula de Hoya. *(with a heavy castilian lisp)* We lived in Barthelona, a thity renowned for its thpithy cuithine.

MADELEINE. Ah Thpain. The bullfights, the flamenco dancers.

OATSIE. And the magnificent cathedrals. One of my great passions is collecting models of the crucifixtion. *(She takes out a cross.)* This Condesa is a Florentine cross, blessed by the brothers of Santa Giovanna. *(The two vampires recoil and twitch with frenzy. RENEE awakes.)*

KING. Ah Renee, my precious.

RENEE. I must have been dreaming. I dreamt I was being devoured by a horrid black bat. *(see MADELEINE and screams)* It was you, it was you!

MADELEINE. Can't you shut her up?

OATSIE. You can't shut out the truth.

MADELEINE. What the...*(She turns to OATSIE. OATSIE flashed the cross at her causing MADELEINE'S hips to bump like a burlesque stripper.)*

OATSIE. I've studied your evil legends all my life. I know you both very well but you don't know me. Let me introduce myself. *(She flings her coat open and throws it to the floor, revealing a man's military jacket covered with medals and polkadotted boxer shorts. She throws off her hat and wig uncovering a shining bald pate. In a thick German dialect.)* I am Gregory Salazar, vampire hunter! God in all of his mercy has cast me in the role of avenging angel to rid the world of your filth.

LA CONDESA. You silly little man, you have no power over us. You shall long be dust while we are forever young. *(He shows her the cross and she too begins to twitch wildly.)*

SALAZAR. At this very moment, the Los Angeles police are surrounding this mansion. The fire department is spraying the walls with holy water. We've got you cornered. Daughters of Lucifer, your reign of death is over. We shall hold you both in this room until the sun rises, the sun which will transform you both into ancient hags and then decaying skeletons and then dust. I will sweep the dust into the gutter with the rest of the swill. From there your remains will float down the pipes into the public sewer where no one will know the difference between your ashes and the rest of the waste products of the Greater Los Angeles Area.

MADELEINE. La Condesa, have you the power to evoke the cry of the banshee?

LA CONDESA. I know the ritual but I've never a-chieved it.

SALAZAR. You do not frighten us with your primitive black magic.

LA CONDESA/MADELEINE.
Flee from Hades, spirits rare.
We free you from your devils lair,
Paint our victims a deep blood red,
Banshees, phantoms, vampires dead.

SALAZAR. Breathe your last, Brides of Beelzebub!

LA CONDESA/MADELEINE.
Far, far into the night
Remove this enemy from our sight
Burn his flesh till it's black with char,
The vampire killer, Salazar!
(SALAZAR'S face grows grotesque as he writhers in agony.)

KING. Look at his face! Flee, Sister, Flee! *(The two vampiresses exit as RENEE unleashes a bloodcurdling scream.)*

SCENE THREE

Las Vegas, today. A rehearsal room at Caesars Palace. Two chorus boys, ZACK and P.J. enter in rehearsal clothes.

ZACK. Hey don't be nervous, man. Mellow out.

P.J. Mellow out? Easier said than done. I'm swallowing razor blades. You'd think I'd never been a chorus gypsy before. It's this town that's giving me the jitters.

ZACK. P.J., you're gonna love Las Vegas. It's the greatest place on earth.

P.J. Besides Transylvania.

ZACK. What do you mean by that?

P.J. Haven't you read in the papers about the string of vampire attacks on the Vegas strip?

ZACK. Who hasn't? But hell, why should you worry? All the victims were young girls.

P.J. Vampires drink the blood of young virgins, right? As the song goes "Take Me Back to Manhattan."

ZACK. Don't let this vampire thing get you down. Hey, give me a Vegas floorshow any day over some tired Broadway trip. And this isn't any ordinary floorshow. Do you know what the name Madeleine Andrews spells?

P.J. *(spelling it out)* M-A-D...

ZACK. No doofus, it spells class. She's one hell of a lady.

P.J. But she hasn't made a movie since the sixties.

ZACK. She did a TV movie two years ago where she played an insane millionairess who owns the Bermuda triangle and steals the shroud of Turin. It cleaned up in the Neilsons. Don't spread this around but she may be starring in a Broadway revival of "The Sound of Music". Play your cards right and you may be employed for a long, long time.

(DANNY enters.)

ZACK. But take this tip, Buddy, stay away from the queens in this company.

DANNY. I heard that, Miss Zack. Stay away from the queens, indeed. Sweetie, has Miss Thing invited you to her dungeon room? Or did I arrive too soon?

ZACK. Fuck off, Mary.

P.J. Hey guys, come on. Miss Andrews will be here any minute.

DANNY. I hope she is. It's about time she discovered this one's true colors.

ZACK. Jealousy, jealousy, jealousy.

DANNY. If you're referring to the one night we slept together. I'd talk about your cock but I've got respect for the dead.

ZACK. You goddamn....*(ZACK tries to attack DANNY but P.J. stops them.)*

P.J. Hey guys, come on, can't you discuss this calmly?

DANNY. I'll tell you what's going on. I've been dancing in Madeleine Andrews' Vegas act for five years. Before that I was a dancer on her TV Variety Show. I've paid my dues with that broad. My lover David has been with her just as long. Then Mata Hari here joins the company and tries to turn her against us.

ZACK. First we have vampires on the strip, now I've got an hysterical faggot to deal with.

DANNY. I wouldn't be worried about vampires, Whorina. Your ass is hardly virgin territory.

ZACK. Don't give me your beads. Your boyfriend's a drunk, he missed a show and Madeleine fired him.

DANNY. You didn't have to squeal on him.

ZACK. Boo hoo.

P.J. Shh, Madeleine's going to hear you!

(MADELEINE ANDREWS enters. It is of course ASTARTE, now the epitome of the glacial, terrifying star of stage, screen, video and Vegas.)

MADELEINE. Hello boys, ready to throw the old girl around? It's nice to see everyone on time for a change.

ZACK. Madeleine, this is P.J., the new dancer.

P.J. It's a real thrill working with you, Miss Andrews.

MADELEINE. Call me Madeleine or we'll never get

along. I love my boys and my boys love me, but there is one thing I will not tolerate and that is drinking or drugs. Is that clear?

P.J. Yes, Miss Andrews.

MADELEINE. *(laughingly)* I told you to call me Madeleine. *(slaps him)* You're cute. Danny, aren't you going to say good morning?

DANNY. Is that quite necessary, Madeleine?

MADELEINE. You bet your sweet ass it is. Now Danny, I'm sure you're very upset that I was forced to fire David but where this show is concerned, I am ruthless. It's my reputation on the line. If Caesars Palace is willing to fork over fifty smackers a week, I better damn well be worth it and that goes for everyone in this clambake. Got me?

EVERYONE. Yes, Madeleine.

MADELEINE. I detest being a boss lady. It's so unattractive. Danny, I'm very fond of you, I'd like to give you some good advice. You're better off without him.

DANNY. Madeleine, I don't want to sound rude but...

MADELEINE. Listen to Mama. You want to be a star?

DANNY. *(sullenly)* Yeah.

MADELEINE. Take this advice. You can't have it all. A long time ago, I made up my mind that there were certain things I had to give up on the road to fame. One of those things was personal happiness. Well, let's get to work. I want this new number in by tomorrow night. Think we can do it, Zack?

ZACK. You bet.

MADELEINE. I hope so. I'll freak if I have to go onstage one more time and do that "I Will Survive" medley.

Freddie, put on the playback.

(They do a strenuous dance number. CHARWOMAN enters mopping the floor. It is the CONDESA fallen on hard time.)

MADELEINE. Cut! Cut! Cut! Zack, would you tell the cleaning lady we're rehearsing.

ZACK. *(to the CONDESA)* Miss, excuse me. We're rehearsing in here. You'll have to come back later.

LA CONDESA. Look bub, I take my orders from Sol Weisenbloom.

ZACK. You don't understand. Madeleine Andrews is rehearsing.

LA CONDESA. Look kid, if I don't get this floor done, my ass will be in a sling.

MADELEINE. Perhaps I can be of some assistance. I'm Madeleine Andrews. *(MADELEINE walks over to the CONDESA, recognizes her and screams in shock.)*

ZACK. Madeleine, are you all right? You look as if you've seen a ghost.

MADELEINE. *(trying to compose herself)* I believe I have. Zack, I'm not quite ready to rehearse.

ZACK. Sure, Madeleine. Whatever you say. Hey guys, let's go get a coke. *(The boys exit.)* We'll be just outside.

MADELEINE. *(with great phoniness)* Zack, I love you. *(ZACK exits.)*

LA CONDESA. La Astarté as I live and breathe. Looks like you're in the chips.

MADELEINE. Can't complain. But what happened to your fortune?

LA CONDESA. Bad investments.

MADELEINE. What brings you here to Vegas?

LA CONDESA. Showgirls. You know I was always a sucker for a shapely gam.

MADELEINE. You've certainly been indiscreet. You've given the Vegas press vampires on the brain.

LA CONDESA. What, have you suddenly switched to artificial plasma? With you it's always the same tune, I'm the monster, you're the victim. My head reels when I think what you did to the girl scout troupe in forty-two. You bounced Hitler off the front page that week.

MADELEINE. Scandal rags. I learned my lesson from that one. Never again will I jeopardize my career. Now when I look for virgins I drive my jaguar beyond the city limits.

(TRACY, a very perky blonde aspiring singer enters.)

TRACY. Madeleine, are you busy?

LA CONDESA. Oh don't mind me, come right in. Are you a new addition to Madeleine's act?

TRACY. Oh, I hope so. I'm Madeleine's latest protegé.

LA CONDESA. Wherever did you two meet? Here in Vegas or beyond the city limits?

TRACY. Oh right here in Vegas. I've been on tour with the Young Republican First Christian College Revue.

MADELEINE. Tracy, what is it you wanted to ask me?

TRACY. Which song do you think would be better for me to sing in your act, "I Enjoy Being a Girl" or "I Hate Men"? And also, how long do I sing before you bite my neck?

LA CONDESA. Please explain that bit of choreography.

TRACY. It's a special Halloween extravaganza. Madeleine appears as a glamorous lady vampire and...

LA CONDESA. I get the general idea. Madeleine. considering all the vampire business in the news, don't you think this could be constructed as being in bad taste?

MADELEINE. Darling, she may have a point, let's keep that part of the act to ourselves. Kind of like a surprise.

TRACY. Sure thing. Well, I'll let you get back to your rehearsal. Tootles. *(TRACY exits.)*

LA CONDESA. You lousy hyocrite. My blood simmers with hatred for you.

MADELEINE. You're just full of venom, aren't you? Look at your face in the glass. For two thousand years you've worn the same expression. Do you know what that is? You're smelling shit. You always look like you're smelling shit. Everywhere you go, you smell shit. Lady, that's your problem. My kind always smells the roses.

LA CONDESA. You don't smell too many roses in Siberia.

MADELEINE. What are you flapping your gums about?

LA CONDESA. 1952. You convinced me to take over your tour of "I Remember Mama". When we got to the Soviet Union, you had me arrested as a CIA spy.

MADELEINE. I never.

LA CONDESA. You did. While you were starting a new career in the movies, I was freezing my ass off in that Gulag.

MADELEINE. 1964. I was top contender for the Oscar. Nick the Greek had me winning ten to one, yet I lost it. Don't think I don't know it was you who spread those filthy rumors that I was boffing Mahalia Jackson.

LA CONDESA. Honey, you got it all wrong. You're the one who's been persecuting me. Me! You've been obsessed with me for two thousand years!

MADELEINE. *(with intense emotion)* Yes, I'm obsessed with you. You made me what I am. Do you think I can ever forgive you for turning me into this, this thing that has no human feeling, this creature who thinks of nothing but her own survival, clawing and attacking anyone who poses a threat to me? Yes, I'm at the top of my profession but I'm not so damn proud of it.

LA CONDESA. Excuse me but I've got a floor to clean.

MADELEINE. Last year, Liv Ullmann and I toured Africa for UNICEF. While I was in the Congo, I left Liv one day and visited a tribal witch doctor named Pooji Dung.

LA CONDESA. *(alarmed)* Pooji Dung?

MADELEINE. I see the name is familiar. He comes from an ancient line of jungle sorcerers. La Condesa, he has taught me all I need know to destroy you.

LA CONDESA. So what do you expect me to do, scream, run around in circles? Do it, get out your voodoo dolls. This modern world stinks. Broadway's dead. You can't get a decent bialy. I've had it. Give me the jungle phase out. You'll be doing me a favor.

MADELEINE. *(chanting)*
Neemy Tunka Seevy Ra.
Keemy Funga Lami Ga.

LA CONDESA. But let me say this. When I'm gone, then will you be happy?

MADELEINE. Feemy, feemy, feemy ragoola. Eemana, eemana, Koorary, ragu...ragu...*(on the verge of hysteria)* Seemy nagu...*(collapses to the floor)* I can't! I can't kill you! Then I shall be truly alone. I've shed a tear. I feel something. Is it impossible that in this whole world, there is only you with whom I can travel through time?

LA CONDESA. *(tough)* Save it for Valentines Day.

MADELEINE. *(simply)* I need you.

LA CONDESA. *(touched)* You need me. Someone needs me?

MADELEINE. In an odd way, your presence has always been a comfort.

LA CONDESA. *(in reverie)* You need me. I am needed.

MADELEINE. Isn't that what life's all about? Funny. *(trying to compose herself)* I'd better get back to rehearsal. What will you do now?

LA CONDESA. I hear at the All Souls Mission they're handing out free grub.

MADELEINE. Surely, you don't mean...Is there anything I can do?

LA CONDESA. Nah.

MADELEINE. No really. Anything. Anything I can do, ten dollars, a warm coat.

LA CONDESA. Yeah, sure. I'd like to have one more shot at stardom. What can I say, I'm crazy for show business.

MADELEINE. Then my girl, you shall be in show business.

LA CONDESA. A comeback?

MADELEINE. A spectacular comeback.' Let me give that to you.

LA CONDESA. But it's been so long. I haven't done anything since "Love American Style" in sixty-seven. I'd be terrified.

MADELEINE. We'll do an act together and we'll break it in in Tahoe. From there we'll hit San Francisco, Los Angeles, Chicago, Boston, the Kennedy Center and then Broadway!

LA CONDESA. Oh boy, the two of us singing and dancing up a storm. And we won't even think about the past.

MADELEINE. What past? At this moment we're the youngest chorines in town.

LA CONDESA. One more thing, dear, a small detail and something that really should be handled by lawyers and not us, nothing to get in the way of our deep friendship. But how do you see my billing in the act?

MADELEINE. *(laughing at the irony of it all)* Dear heart, I can see it all. Glittering letters thirty feet high. Tonight on the great stage, Madeleine Andrews, Magda Legerdemain, the legendary, the notorious, love 'em or hate 'em, the Vampire Lesbians of Sodom!

(The two ladies explode in laughter. The music swells covering their enthusiastic voices as they begin rehearsing a dance step for their new act.)

CURTAIN

COSTUME PLOT

SLEEPING BEAUTY or COMA

MISS THICK:
Scene One and Two:
> wool suit

Scene Eight:
> gold lame mini-skirt and jacket

Scene Nine:
> ripped and distressed safari suit

ENID:
Scene One thru Six:
> mini-skirted jumper, blouse and tie, shoulder length blonde wig, black tights

Scene Three and Four:
> plastic rain slicker

Scene Seven:
> full length cape, long breakaway skirt, and matching mini-dress

Scene Eight:
> pink body stocking, mini-dress made of pink and black plastic tiles, wig made of mylar spirals

Scene Nine:
> full length bathrobe, long blonde wig, stylish contemporary white short dress, modern styled blonde wig

78

SEBASTIAN:

Scene One, Two:

> pink suit, pink shoes, lavendar shirt, polka dot tie, white pompadour wig

Scene Eight:

> orange Nehru jacket, paisley bell bottom pants, medallion, white page boy wig

Scene Nine:

> distressed safari suit and helmet

FAUNA:

Scene One:

> paisley print sack dress smock, white hose, pink shoes, short dark brown wig

Scene Four — Seven:

> black velvet mini-dress with white satin collar, black shoes

Scene Eight:

> lamé mini-dress with bare midriff connected by gold chains, pink shoes, long brown wig

Scene Nine:

> long black cape, black hat with veil, white sequined mini-dress, bracelets, rhinestone earrings saying 86, spiked out dark wig

IAN:

Scene One, Four, Five, Six:

> orange turtleneck, off white corduroy pants, brown boots, brown velvet cap

Scene Eight:

> Sergeant Pepper jacket

Scene Nine:
> red leather jacket, red jeans, T-shirt

ANTHEA:
Scene One:
> yellow Chanel-type suit with matching pillbox hat, black wig with flip

Scene Eight:
> lime green cocktail dress with chiffon overlay dotted with orange pompoms, black mod hairdo

BARRY:
Scene Eight:
> red satin shirt, gold chain necklace, black bellbottoms, black afro wig

CRAIG:
Scene Nine:
> red exercise sweat suit

PROTESTERS:
Scene Three:
> white pants, white shirts decorated with dayglo paint, Pierott masks, black derbys, top hats and a Union Jack flag in one of their pockets

PROPERTY LISTS

SLEEPING BEAUTY or COMA

SCENE ONE:
models photos
fashion sketches
a bolt of fabric
a doorbell

SCENE THREE:
two London Times newspapers
three pairs of Groucho glasses
two signs on poles saying "Now is Here!" and "Down
    With No!"
a butterfly net

SCENE FOUR:
an umbrella

SCENE FIVE:
a bouquet of flowers

SCENE SIX:
bottle of nail polish
a camera

SCENE EIGHT:
a bottle of Guinness Beer
five champagne glasses
a box labeled LSD

SCENE NINE:
a wheel chair
a hypodermic needle

COSTUME PLOT

VAMPIRE LESBIANS OF SODOM

ALI:
Scene One:
>sandals, breakaway gold loin cloth, G-string, matching head and armbands

HUJAR:
Scene One:
>sandals, gold loin cloth, head and armbands

VIRGIN SACRIFICE:
Scene One:
>flowing red wig to waist, Tulle hip wrap with large bow in front, spike heels, flowered wreath in hair

SUCCUBUS:
Scene One:
>outrageous wig, corselette, panties, tights, chiffon cape, spike heels, black lace gloves

LA CONDESA:
Scene Two:
>gold and black beaded floorlength twenties gown, jeweled choker, black headress with plumes, spike heels, black lace gloves

Scene Three:
>grey wig, distressed skirt, blouse, cardigan sweater, bedroom slippers

MADELEINE:

Scene Two:

red wig, rhinestone tiara with mauve plumes, elegant mauve lace twenties gown with train, matching hose, gloves and shoes, jeweled choker, rhinestone earrings, ropes of pearls

Scene Three:

sequined man tailored shirt, tights, spike heels, choker, earrings and outrageous red bouffant wig

RENEE:

Scene Two:

white Mary Pickford dress with pink sash, pink shoes, long black wig with pink bow

KING:

Scene Two:

black pants, white dinner jacket, tie

ETIENNE:

Scene Two:

black tails, red bowtie, cummerbund, black shoes

OATSIE:

Scene Two:

flamboyant twenties full length coat with ruffled collar, high heels, large picture hat, blonde wig, glasses on a chain, hose. (as Salazar) bald pate, military jacket with sash and medals, white boxer shorts with red polka dots

P.J.:
Scene Three:
   gym shorts, tank top, jazz shoes

ZACH:
Scene Three:
   jazz pants, midriff top, jazz shoes

DANNY:
Scene Three:
   jazz pants, tank top, headband, jazz shoes

TRACY:
Scene Three:
   blonde wig, short rehearsal skirt and top, jazz
   shoes

PROPERTY LIST

VAMPIRE LESBIANS OF SODOM

Scene Two:
> Etienne's red handkerchief
> doorbell
> a crucifix

Scene Three:
> a mop

PLOT SYNOPSES

SLEEPING BEAUTY or COMA

London, 1966. A kooky young girl named Enid is discovered by the meglomaniacal fashion designer, Sebastian Loré, to be his top model. She escapes his clutches and joins forces with a struggling young designer named Fauna and her photographer boyfriend, Ian. The three friends become the rage of swinging mod London. Sebastian exacts his revenge by slipping Enid some bad LSD, plunging her into a deep coma. Fifteen years later, a handsome nutritionist injects the sleeping beauty with megadoses of vitamins. Enid awakes and she and her devoted friends all live happily ever after.

VAMPIRE LESBIANS OF SODOM

In ancient Sodom, a young girl is sacrificed to the dreaded Succubus, a beautiful vampiress who thrives on the blood of young girls. Through a trick of fate, the girl is transformed into a vampire and plots her revenge. They meet again in 1920's Hollywood, where the Succubus, now known as Magda Legerdemain, is a silent screen vamp. The virgin appears as Madeleine Astarté, a rival star. A lady gossip columnist arrives to interview them and reveals herself to be a male vampire hunter. The two ladies defeat their enemy and flee. In 1980's Las Vegas, Madeleine is now a hardboiled headliner. She meets up again with Magda, reduced to being a charwoman. They rekindle their feud until they realize that in this cold modern world, all they really have is each other.

Other Publications for Your Interest

COMING ATTRACTIONS
(ADVANCED GROUPS—COMEDY WITH MUSIC)

By TED TALLY, music by JACK FELDMAN, lyrics by BRUCE SUSSMAN and FELDMAN

5 men, 2 women—Unit Set

Lonnie Wayne Burke has the requisite viciousness to be a media celebrity—but he lacks vision. When we meet him, he is holding only four people hostage in a laundromat. There aren't any cops much less reporters around, because they're across town where some guy is holding *50* hostages. But, a talent agent named Manny sees possibilities in Lonnie Wayne. He devises a criminal persona for him by dressing him in a skeleton costume and sending him door-to-door, murdering people as "The Hallowe'en Killer". He is captured, and becomes an instant celebrity, performing on TV shows. When his fame starts to wane, he crashes the Miss America Pageant disguised as Miss Wyoming to kill Miss America on camera. However, he falls in love with her, and this eventually leads to his downfall. Lonnie ends up in the electric chair, and is fried "live" on prime-time TV as part of a jazzy production number! "Fizzles with pixilated laughter."—Time. "I don't often burst into gales of laughter in the theatre; here, I found myself rocking with guffaws."—New York Mag. "Vastly entertaining."—Newark Star-Ledger.

(Royalty, $50–$40.)

SORROWS OF STEPHEN
(ADVANCED GROUPS—COMEDY)

By PETER PARNELL

4 men, 5 women—Unit set

Stephen Hurt is a headstrong, impetuous young man—an irrepressible romantic—he's unable not to be in love. One of his models is Goethe's tragic hero, Werther, but as a contemporary New Yorker, he's adaptable. The end of an apparently undying love is followed by the birth of a grand new passion. And as he believes there's a literary precedent for all romantic possibilities justifying his choices—so with enthusiasm bordering on fickleness, he turns from Tolstoy, to Stendhal or Balzac. And Stephen's never discouraged—he can withstand rivers of rejection. (From the N.Y. Times.) And so his affairs—real and tentative—begin when his girl friend leaves him. He makes a romantic stab at a female cab driver, passes an assignation note to an unknown lady at the opera, flirts with an accessible waitress—and then has a tragic-with-comic-overtones, wild affair with his best friend's fiancée. "Breezy and buoyant. A real romantic comedy, sophisticated and sentimental, with an ageless attitude toward the power of positive love."—N.Y. Times.

(Slightly Restricted. Royalty, $50–$40, where available)

Other Publications for Your Interest

KNOCK KNOCK
(LITTLE THEATRE—FARCE)

By JULES FEIFFER

3 men, 1 woman—Composite interior

Take a pair of old Jewish bachelor recluses, throw in Joan of Arc who also in another life was Cinderella—add another character who appears in various guises and you have the entire cast but not the story of this wild farce. Cohn, an atheistic ex-musician is the housekeeper ''half'' of this ''odd couple.'' Abe, an agnostic ex-stockbroker is the practical ''half.'' They have lived together for twenty years—are bored to tears with one another and constantly squabble. Cohn, exasperated, wishes for intelligent company and on the scene enters one Wiseman who appears in many roles and is part Mephistopheles, part Groucho Marx. Then Joan of Arc appears before the couple telling them her mission is to recruit two of every species for a spaceship trip to heaven. After that all antic hell breaks loose and continues to the mad ending. ''. . . a wild spree of jokes . . . helium-light laughter.''—Clive Barnes, N.Y. Times. ''. . . a kooky, laugh-saturated miracle play in the absurdist tradition.''—Time. ''. . . grand fun, possessed by a bright madness . . .''—N.Y. Post. ''. . . a knockout of original humor.''—NBC. ''. . . intelligent and very funny play.''—WABC-TV.

(Royalty, $50-$35.)

LITTLE MURDERS
(ALL GROUPS—COMEDY)

By JULES FEIFFER

6 men, 2 women—Interior

''Jules Feiffer, a satirical sharpshooter with a deadly aim, stares balefully at the meaningless violence in American life, and opens fire on it in 'Little Murders.' . . . Can be devastatingly lethal in some of its coldly savage comic assaults.'' (N.Y. Post). The play is really a collection of what Walter Kerr called set pieces, showing us a modern metropolitan family of matriarchal mother, milquetoast father, normal cuddly sister, and brother who is trying to adapt himself to homosexuality. Sister's fiance is a fellow who knows how to roll with the punches; he figures that if you daydream while being mugged, it won't hurt so much. They have a hard time finding a preacher who will marry them without pronouncing the name of God. But they succeed, to their sorrow. For immediately afterward sister is killed by a sniper's bullet. A detective who has a stack of unsolved crimes suspects that there is ''a subtle pattern'' forming here. '''Little Murders' is fantastically funny. You will laugh a lot.''—N.Y. Times. ''You have made me laugh, you have made me collapse. I want to go back.''—N.Y. Post. ''One of the finest comedies this season.—NBC-TV.

(Royalty, $50-$25.)